EYE OF
THE STORM

EYE OF THE STORM

Personal Commitment to Managing Symptoms of PTSD

Jacqueline Buckley, CD, BA

iUniverse LLC
Bloomington

EYE OF THE STORM
Personal Commitment to Managing Symptoms of PTSD

Copyright © 2014 Jacqueline Buckley, CD, BA.

All rights reserved. No part of this book may be used or reproduced by any means, graphic, electronic, or mechanical, including photocopying, recording, taping or by any information storage retrieval system without the written permission of the publisher except in the case of brief quotations embodied in critical articles and reviews.

iUniverse books may be ordered through booksellers or by contacting:

iUniverse LLC
1663 Liberty Drive
Bloomington, IN 47403
www.iuniverse.com
1-800-Authors (1-800-288-4677)

Because of the dynamic nature of the Internet, any web addresses or links contained in this book may have changed since publication and may no longer be valid. The views expressed in this work are solely those of the author and do not necessarily reflect the views of the publisher, and the publisher hereby disclaims any responsibility for them.

Any people depicted in stock imagery provided by Thinkstock are models, and such images are being used for illustrative purposes only. Certain stock imagery © Thinkstock.

ISBN: 978-1-4917-1825-4 (sc)
ISBN: 978-1-4917-1826-1 (hc)
ISBN: 978-1-4917-1827-8 (e)

Library of Congress Control Number: 2013923058

Printed in the United States of America.

iUniverse rev. date: 01/22/2014

INTRODUCTION

For more than a decade, I have struggled with anxiety and bouts of depression. Regardless of the countless number of times I sought assistance for my symptoms, I was lost in a sea of bureaucracy. I struggled alone—a single parent raising two children, aiming to keep afloat. In my struggle with anxiety symptoms, I became complacent. I was unrecognizable in some ways, losing all sense of who I really was. Compassion faded. Emotions withered. I became like an empty shell whose former inhabitant had departed.

The process of writing this book has been both therapeutic and emotional. I have journeyed for three years to reconnect with my true self and soul. I have cried many tears onto the pages of my writing. I have gotten angry, laughed, and felt joy, pain, and sorrow during my countless edits.

Easy? I think not. When I began writing, I thought the process would be simple. After all, I was born with a creative gift. I had been writing poetry longer than I could remember. I assumed that writing my thoughts on paper and sharing my struggles couldn't be simpler; could it? After all, I have struggled and have overcome huge obstacles. I know how it feels to be at my worst. I should know how to connect and tell my story. That concept has been so far from the truth.

Writing this book has been a process in its own right, but it has been worth my time. It has had both a purpose and a meaning. No matter how many edits. No matter how many hours. If you understand that commitment and struggle can bring us back from the deep, and if that is all you take away from this book, it has been worth it.

It is no surprise that my first entry of this memoir is about the last part of my process in the final stages of my writing. I am excited that I have won, but—more importantly—I'm excited that I am able to share my experience with you. I am excited for you. I have so much faith in knowing that if you commit to yourself and commit to being in your journey beyond your symptoms, you will achieve.

Today is September 1, 2013. Approximately five days ago, I sent an e-mail to my editorial consultant. I share this excerpt from the e-mail:

> I sent you an e-mail a few days ago and said I would be resubmitting Monday, as it's a holiday here and I could concentrate over the weekend and not think about having to go back to work. What is ironic is

Eye of the Storm

that Monday is September 2, which will be fifteen years to the date since Swissair 111 crashed off the shores of Peggy's Cove, the event that led me to write this book.

There is a greater meaning of all things. This is one of them. I had no idea when I sent that e-mail what the meaning would take on. I believe that everything happens for a reason. There are lessons or greater meanings behind events; sometimes we have to look beyond the apparent. The e-mail was one of those instances.

This is a bit of my story. A small portion—but with enough for you to understand. A place where I put my mind, body, and soul back together. Sometimes, when we are in our deepest sorrows, our most difficult moments—the moments when we feel life may not be worth the hassles—remember, the world is more complete with you living in it.

If you get nothing from what I am about to share, I hope you take away my most important message: you are not alone.

Tragedy should be utilized as a source of strength. No matter what sort of difficulties, how painful experience is, if we lose our hope, that's our real disaster. —**Dalai Lama**

I recall the day as if it were yesterday. I walked into Doc K's office and sat down. It began as a normal session about my weekly progress, accomplishments, and revelations of putting pieces together. During that session, I shared an e-mail. It was a conversation between my closest friend's daughter, Clarissa, and me. She was creating the image for my book's cover. At that point, I had tossed a few thoughts for the title and cover around in my head, but none fit. No matter how hard I tried, I was not settled on that aspect of my book. I became frustrated. The more frustrated I became, the more inspiration disappeared.

I explained to Doc K that in order to provide Clarissa with enough clarity on what the book was about, I had told her of how my life had changed over the course of the previous twelve years or so. I described a bit of the event but had left the remaining details in her hands to read about on the Internet. The rest of the e-mail focused on my vision for a cover. It was vague. I wrote, "When creating, perhaps think about things in nature, things that evolve to show death and rebirth. For instance, a wilted rose blooming again because it has been given water. That sort of thing, keeping it symbolic." I left her to her work.

It was at that point that I decided to read the initial e-mail and its reply to Doc K. My goal was to give him a greater sense of why

I was overwhelmed and teary during this session. It seemed to me that I had not been as overwhelmed and teary in other sessions. I began reading the e-mail, and—as always—my emotions took over. This was the first time I had really spoken of posttraumatic stress disorder (PTSD) and how it affected my life. The e-mail was raw and overwhelming; my words connected my heart and my mind together. I was connecting with what I was saying. Sure, I had talked about things to others in the past and outside of my normal therapy sessions, but not in a way that let me really connect the emotions to the event that changed my life. I continued reading the e-mail reply. When I got to the part where Clarissa had written her idea for the cover, I choked up again. Tears streamed down my face, and I could barely catch my breath. She envisioned a seashell on a calm shore. The ocean and the shore had become imprints in my mind for so many years. While the idea gave me chills, I realized right then that the idea was perfect. But it would not be a calm shore, as *calm* had not played a huge role in my life up until more recently.

I expressed to Doc K that I had decided to have Clarissa create the cover setting with gray, stormy skies and a hint of light peeking through the clouds. The shoreline would be recovering from a surge, and the shell amidst it would be all alone and empty. That, in a nutshell, had been my life for many years. Alone in some aspects, but more or less empty. I shared with Doc K that I compare PTSD to a storm. It appears with no warning, plays havoc on all that comes within its path, and then fades out—often leaving things desolate or destroyed.

A few weeks later, as I was driving in a calm, serene state, the words *eye of the storm* suddenly popped into my head. I had no idea why, but I seized the moment and began to think. The eye of the storm is said to be the calmest place that sits in the middle of turmoil. While a storm's rage plays havoc on anything in its path, the eye remains fairly calm, with sunshine and calm winds. For many years, I was the storm surrounding the eye. Now, after nearly three years in treatment, I can say that I am the eye of the storm. Regardless of the uncontrolled turmoil I may encounter, the uncontrollable flashbacks that still occur, or the uncontrollable symptoms that may appear for no apparent reason—as long as I can remain in the eye of the storm where mindfulness controls the eye—I am safe.

WEATHER WARNING

Life seemed normal. But what is normal? I had faced challenges we all encounter at some point in our lives. I had lost loved ones. I had been through the death of my children's father just after our divorce. I had faced the challenges of raising my children as a single parent. Yup, life in my view was normal. I had learned to cope with life's little struggles, and I still don't believe that I have had it any more difficult than the next person. My philosophy on that was—and still is—pretty simple: someone else is going through more difficult situations than me, and I should be thankful.

I don't think I am hallucinating to believe that, at some point in our lives, all of us will encounter difficult times. The way each of us handles our challenges is different, as each of us perceives our circumstances differently. When those difficulties or challenges are upon us, most of us do our best to embrace and cope with situations. We get through them the best we know how. Sometimes difficulties and challenges are ones that we do not plan for. We accept that times

Jacqueline Buckley, CD, BA

may become tough, and we muddle through. When we hear on the news about different tragedies, we become shocked. And if you are anything like me, you may look at the event with the eyes of a stranger. You may even think it will never happen to you.

If events don't affect our families or us, they seem to be just events. We can only imagine the pain. I can sympathize with what I think someone may be dealing with, but—if I haven't lived it—how can I understand the true magnitude of that person's experience?

I have learned and truly believe that even preparing for situations will never give us the true realization of an event. Unless we witness it or experience it for ourselves, we can only imagine what things may be like. Unless we are there, we cannot fully prepare ourselves or appreciate the true meaning of the event—or the effects that it will have on us. We can only assume. We can only speculate or imagine. Our reactions and responses during tragedies of nature, violence, or sudden loss cannot be predetermined. I strongly believe that even the men and women who witness tragedies on a daily basis are not immune to any single event and how that event may affect them at any given time. We are human.

I recall waking in the wee hours on the morning of September 3, 1998, to the sound of sirens and helicopter propellers. The sirens and noise seemed to last for hours. I recall being suddenly filled with anxiety. Living within the perimeters of an air base and the shrill of sirens meant that perhaps something more was happening than the random call of an ambulance. My initial thought was, *Oh my gosh, there must have been a bad crash that was probably vehicle-related.*

Sleep became difficult and the anxiety became worse. The more sirens I heard, the worse I felt. It was a feeling I had never had before. My mind began racing and I could not shut it off. My stomach knotted. I seemed to be preparing for the worst. But what was that?

Later that morning, I drove to work as usual. I carpooled with a few of my coworkers and made my normal round to pick them up. As soon as my second coworker entered the car, I said, "Boy, did you hear all the sirens last night? You'd think there was an airplane crash or something." Nothing could have prepared me for the shocking statement that followed. "There was," Dave said. "A plane crashed in the water just off of Peggy's Cove." I could not believe my ears, but those words would continue to haunt me, along with the events of the next few months.

In the days to follow, teams of professionals and organizations came together to provide support in the recovery and identification of the 229 souls who perished the evening of September 2, 1998, aboard Swissair flight 111.

Tragic events take the physical lives of others, but they also often take the emotional lives of those who play humanitarian or peacekeeping roles. I would become one of those victims, haunted by the unconscious memories and imprints of the tragedy.

As a member of the Canadian Forces Dental Services stationed in Halifax, Nova Scotia, I was tasked with assisting our dental officers in the dental forensic portion of the recovery. I am not sure what I was thinking when we were told we would be assisting in the recovery. My thoughts focused on survivors, and even if we had had to deal with the deceased, I can tell you nothing would have prepared me for what I saw.

A morgue was constructed within one of the hangars at Canadian Forces Base Shearwater. Another hangar became the home for the wreckage pieces. Inside the morgue hangar, they built temporary rooms—similar to hospital rooms. They contained steel tables, x-ray viewers, and tables for equipment. Our unit brought in our dental vans. They were equipped with a sterilizer, dental supplies, and x-ray equipment.

I recall the first day I was expected to report to the hangar. As I walked in, I was nervous. The smell was strange, and I had no idea what to expect or where to go. The hangar and its contents were unfamiliar. I remember signing in and making my way around to our dental operation. There were a few tables on the hangar floor near our dental van. The faces of coworkers were the only familiar sights.

Beyond the main floor area was the normal office area within the hangar. This area would become the dental identification area for the dental officers. During my exposure therapy years later, I would relive the memories of this hangar by looking at photographs.

I don't recall much from that first day. Memories are scattered, but the days to follow would tell a different story. Some memories stayed with me for more than a decade.

Time would embrace me with nightmares and both visual and olfactory flashbacks. As I look back now over the past years, I realize that my mind prepared me for something different.

During our briefing, prior to going into that atmosphere, I had mentally prepared myself for seeing survivors—or at the very least recognizing intact bodies. With a pre-military background as a nurse's assistant, I had no concerns about seeing death. But I had not prepared myself for the aftermath of this horrific accident.

Sitting and waiting became a common theme. While crews were out in the water recovering remnants of the aftermath, we sat and waited for their return. Time seemed to tick slowly. Then I received an assignment. I was asked to take an x-ray. That x-ray would be of a tooth still attached to a small fragment of bone and tissue. Nothing more. There was no recognizable person, just a part of a person who once was. This would become the norm.

In the following days, more and more remains entered the morgue. As I observed the contents of each body bag with the medics, dentists, and doctors, my mind automatically related everything to a horror movie and props. My mind switched off, and I became numb. I was in the process of fight and survival. I had no idea. I have been told that there is an onset or trigger moment that begins the process of PTSD. I have since learned that this is perhaps where my point began.

I recall sitting on the dental van stairs awaiting another assignment. I seemed to sit in that location a lot when I could. I don't know why. The assignment came. A partial torso was recovered, and my assignment was to assist in removing the dental remains still attached. As I approached the door to the room, my heart sank, and the pit of my stomach filled with horror. I was dazed and stood in shock. I can still barely recall the disfigurement of the head—but I do recall seeing body hair—and then it hit me. This is a *real person*. These are not movie props. I shut off at that instant. I waited as they cut the small amount of the remaining jaws. Then I held out my hand as a piece was handed to me to begin the x-raying process. I became an emotional zombie.

Even today, I can still see and feel that exact moment in time. We have discovered through the therapy process that this was probably my catalyst point.

I have sat in Doc K's office many times and discussed this scene. I have often had flashbacks of this gentleman, and my mind always retreats back to the same question. *Who was he?* I am convinced that if I knew the answer to that question, if I could put a name to the person, I would be able to make sense of it all. I believe that knowing who he was and where he was from would allow me to connect the part of me that still is somewhat in disbelief. As I write these words, I am crying. I want to grieve normally, but somehow that part of my grieving is missing. While my heart believes this was real, my mind cannot connect to the facts. I cry, yet I am confused.

When I talk of him, I feel like a part of me is missing. I continue to ask questions. Even though I had witnessed other body parts and pieces, none were more recognizable than him. The arm, the hair, the jewelry—all vague pieces of a puzzle. I still have difficulty wondering if they were real, or if they were parts I imagined. When I remember, I become frustrated. If only I knew who he was.

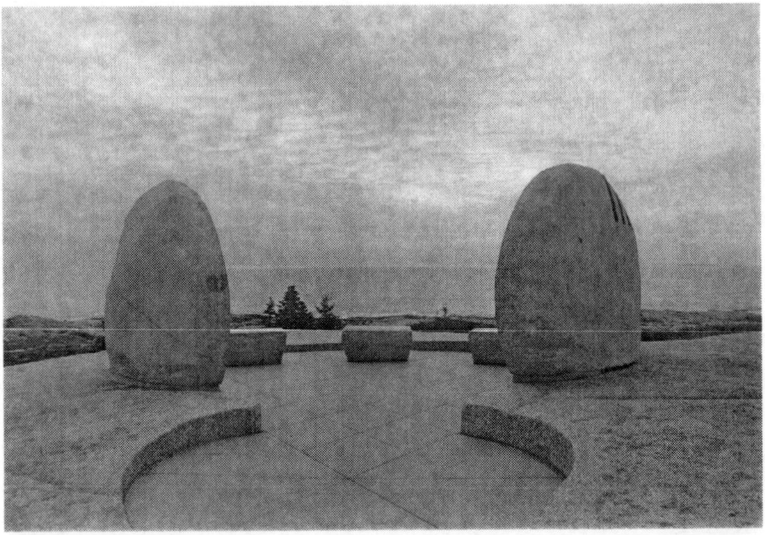

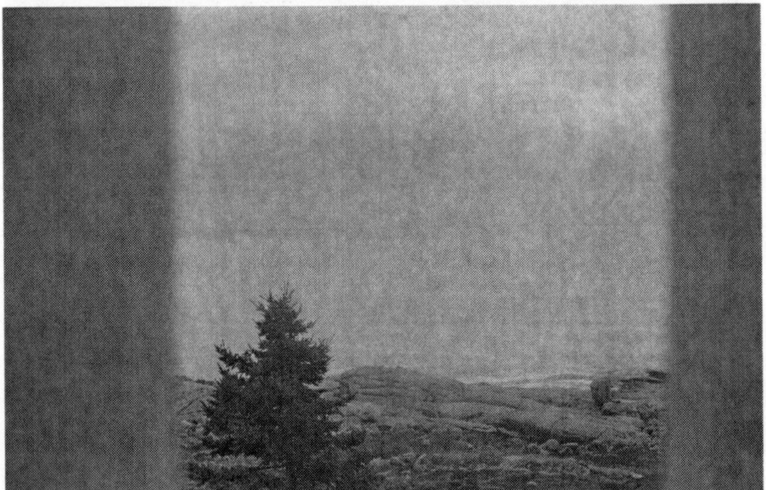

Photos:

Top: Swissair Memorial at Peggy's Cove, Nova Scotia. (2011)

Bottom: The middle landmark point of the crash through the memorial windows. Each of the window slats in the memorial represents a landmark point of the entire crash site, creating a triangle. This window shows the top peak of that triangle. (2011)

Although the world is full of suffering, it is also full of the overcoming of it.—**Helen Keller**

STORM

"Posttraumatic stress disorder or PTSD is a severe anxiety disorder that can occur after someone has been exposed to any event that leaves him or her with psychological trauma. It can result from exposure to events that leave intense negative feelings such as fear, helplessness, and horror for the event's participant or the observer."[1]

I am not a physician, physiologist, or researcher. I would, however, consider myself a personal expert on the topic—based on my own account, recollections, and symptoms living with PTSD for more than fourteen years. My most recollected moments are focused on the past two and a half years while I have been in active treatment for its symptoms. During that time, I have learned more about PTSD and its symptoms through my own personal battles and triumphs. I have worked extremely hard

---

[1] "Posttraumatic Stress Disorder," *Wikipedia*, [add access date here], http://en.wikipedia.org/wiki/Posttraumatic stress disorder.

in my own recovery. I have learned to manage my symptoms and retrain my thought process. I have developed my own strategies to manage my symptoms.

What I can share with you is real. It is a raw account of my own healing, observations, and understanding. My strategies and suggestions are based on what has worked for me; they may or may not work for you. I know they have worked for me. And I will explain *why* they have worked in a later chapter. I have approached things during treatment based on the ideals that any suggestion given to me was merely a suggestion. If I decided to try what was being suggested and it worked, then great. If I didn't try, then I would never know the outcome. I had nothing to lose by trying. If I tried and gained nothing, I lost nothing. Every moment toward the management of symptoms—regardless of success—was, in fact, not lost time. Lost time is living the same way you have and doing nothing to improve or change your circumstances. Lost time is always complaining about things and never making that change. One thing I have learned is that when I have applied these strategies, they have worked.

I am a strong believer that someone who has lived through an experience can often provide you with greater detail of the event than someone who has not lived it. The emotion is a true account of what they felt and encountered.

I believe that even though many people may experience the same circumstances, each will have different perceptions of what they encountered. Therefore, the information they share will be different from person to person.

I believe that research is done on specific topics to give an overview of the topic researched. However, you can have two individuals researching the same topic and both may come out with a different hypothesis. I have discovered through the years that each type of treatment I have encountered has been subjective. This depended on the diagnosis I was provided by that particular individual. I was given so many different diagnoses over the years—and I encountered so many health-care practitioners—that some days I didn't know if I was coming or going. I engaged in different therapy techniques and never made any progress. I became frustrated.

Because I was in the military, things and people constantly changed. My health-care providers changed on a regular basis, and I became tired of the revolving door. Each time I began a routine for treatment, either I (or the individual I was seeing) would move, and I would have to start the process over again. PTSD comes with enough of its own symptoms that cause stress, so the last thing I needed was more stress added on to the pile.

Jacqueline Buckley, CD, BA

During the past few years, I have tried my own different techniques and strategies along with the commitment of therapy. I have found ways to improve my thought process and even minimize the dramatization of my symptoms when they appear without warning. Working on symptom management in a controlled forum of the therapy office is much different than when you have symptoms while you are alone. *Scary* can often take on a life of its own when symptoms hit and you are in the midst of a crowd or around family.

I have learned that it is imperative to find a health-care provider who not only understands PTSD, but also who continuously researches it and perhaps has made it the focus of his or her practice. I have been fortunate that even though it took nearly twelve years to find such a person, I finally did. But one key point that I have also discovered in the process is that we need to be accountable to ourselves, and we need to find our own coping mechanisms between our appointments. This does not include self-medicating with things and practices that can become addictive or harmful to others or us. I am talking about healthy practices, such as reading, exercise, yoga, meditation, or even a hobby. Regardless of whichever self-care technique we choose, everything should be done in moderation and with balance.

Eye of the Storm

In a nutshell, am I optimistic that if you commit, change your thought process from *might* to *will*, are optimistic, and believe that changing some things in your life will make a difference for you, then you can get through your trauma? Absolutely. You have to remember I had been living with symptoms for nearly eleven years before I was diagnosed, and I still live with them today. The difference today is how I manage those symptoms when they occur. I know I can manage them without being fearful. My techniques and tricks may assist you, or they might not. It is all in your perception of the message. The choice is yours. They worked for me, so why would they not work for you unless you make no effort? There is an old saying that if you want to make changes in your life, you will actually have to change what you are already doing. Change begins within us, and if we honestly *want* change, we will make it happen. If we don't make it happen, we are not distressed enough to make those changes.

Focus on where you want to go, not on what you fear.—**Anthony Robbins**

THE VORTEX

One of the biggest obstacles in my life has been fear. It has stopped me from standing up for myself when I felt weak. It has stopped me from being in places that made me uncomfortable. It has stopped me from trying new foods. It has stopped me from going to my medical appointments. It has stopped me from getting on a plane. The list could go on. Fear is what stood in the way of my enjoying life. I was sometimes too afraid to even step outside my own home. Not because I was afraid to be outside, but because I was afraid I would have a panic attack in public. Silly as it may sound, I was worried about it all the time, and then it happened.

My daughter was attending school half days in Calgary. I would drive her in the morning for classes and pick her up at noon. My routine was simple. I would drop her off and head over to the local Smitty's for coffee and toast. Then I would browse around or run errands until it was time to pick her up.

One day, I had decided to go to the mall where Doc K's office had been. I browsed around for a while in the stores and decided it was time to leave. I was giving myself enough time to get back to the school. As I walked through the mall heading toward the exit, I encountered a sharp pain in the middle of my back. It lasted but a mere second and then was gone. Immediately, the panic mode hit. My heart began racing. *Oh no*, I thought. *This is not happening.* I made it to my car and began driving. My thoughts were going faster than I was driving. *I'm having a heart attack*, I thought. *Why won't my heart stop racing so fast? No*, I thought. *It's a panic attack. I should be able to slow down my heart. I should be able to breathe normally.* The more I thought, the more my symptoms escalated.

I tried to call my husband. I thought that if I could at least talk to him that I would be able to take my mind and focus elsewhere. I needed to be mindful. I needed to get control of the situation. Each time I would calm myself down a little, it would start all over again.

Finally I reached the school and decided I would wait inside. I at least figured that if it were my heart, I would not be in my car alone. After all, my first aid classes taught me that much. I sat down and waited, but my heart was still racing. Finally, I decided to say something to the receptionist. "I don't feel well," I stated. "I think it's my heart." She asked if she should call 911 and before I knew what was happening, I was being greeted by firemen, a blood pressure cuff, and two children's aspirin. *Oh, great*, I thought. *I have a medication fear, and now I am being faced with that, too. Terrific.*

From the firemen to the back of an ambulance, off I went to the nearest emergency room. *For a panic attack?* I was hooked up to an IV, had electrodes attached to every part of my skin—and let's not forget the blood donation. For the next four hours, I sat and was monitored. Best of all, I now had even more reason to fear going outside.

Well, I survived that day despite how I may have felt at the time. I got over the embarrassment of causing such a scene. Most importantly, I learned that I had survived and thrived. Yes, I had a fear of having a panic attack—and yes, the worst-case scenario had happened—but I had made it through. I had overcome my fear and I was okay. I learned something very valuable that day. I learned that my fear was based on other people's perceptions of how I thought they would perceive me.

You see, while I was employed in the military, I heard the words *suck it up, princess* and *just get on with it* more than enough times. It seemed like common statements made whenever I showed any type of vulnerability to my peers. I was perceived to be weak, not dependable, and not leader material. My perceptions were based on comments like these, and as a result I learned to conform to my environment.

During the years shortly after the incident, I attended medical appointments on a regular basis. When I would return to work, I was told that I was not dependable and reliable. I was not putting the organization first. I believed that attending too many appointments showed a lack of initiative. I believed that not putting the organization first or taking care of myself and my health could then lead to the loss of a promotion opportunity or even poor performance reviews. I replayed the voice of others inside my head and convinced myself that I was okay even when I was not. I felt intimidated and weak. I was worried about how I would be perceived by my supervisors. As a result, my mental and physical health deteriorated. I was living with a fear of being judged by others.

I also began missing opportunities because of that fear. The biggest opportunity was the one of fighting for myself and for my health. Sadly, I did not realize that fear existed in my own mind. When I realized what fears lived within me, I was able to understand them. Rather than fighting against them or avoiding them, I worked with them. I took a deeper look into the reasons behind them.

For example, I loved to fly. I could recall days when being on a plane excited me. The

Eye of the Storm

more turbulence, the better. I never associated anything negative with flying. I was not fearful. In fact, it was my love of planes that had drawn me to the military. I had dreams of being an aircraft mechanic for the Snowbirds.

After 1998, I began to avoid flying. Just the thought of flying created an uneasy, unsettling, and sick pit in my stomach. I became anxious, white knuckled, and often teary when any bout of turbulence began. My heart raced and my breathing changed. I could feel the sweat in the palms of my hands. I would rub my legs and fidget in my seat. Thoughts about jumping out even crossed my mind. Just think about that for a second. Thirty-some-odd thousand feet in the air—I pop out the door and what? I am going to spread my arms and flap my way back to the ground? I had no rationale. Only after I realized this was a huge fear was I was able to talk about it in a way that let me work at finding a solution for either overcoming it in the moment or conquering it fully.

My husband and I love Florida. We have made it our special place. It is our place of relaxation. We try to return each year, and each year I know we have to fly. If we don't fly, chances are when we get there we will be turning around and driving back the same day. That has not been an option for me. I love the Florida weather. Even thinking about it while

21

writing makes me happy inside. I can even smell and feel the air on my skin, and I have not even left Alberta.

A few years back, we had the trip planned. Having been in the midst of treatment, my anxiety was over the roof. I discussed the trip with Doc K, and he suggested that when or if turbulence hit, I should close my eyes and focus as if the plane were surfing a wave, like in a boat. I was not fearful of boats or water, and the concept seemed rational. My initial thoughts when he suggested this were, *Umm, okay, you want me to forget planes but think about water? The same water that I associated with planes? Okay, you jerk.* Well, regardless of how crazy that sounded, it worked. Now when I fly, I refocus my thoughts when turbulence hits, and I no longer want to jump out—at least not without a parachute. Each trip is different. I conquer each one at a time. I focus on other things, rather than the one thing I can't control once we have taken off.

When I began the process of treatment for PTSD, I was sick and tired of being sick and tired. I was both physically and mentally drained. I had no emotional feeling except anger. I knew how to cry but did not know why I was crying. When I was asked what I was feeling, I would often respond with "I don't know, sort of cold." I learned that I was disassociating from

Eye of the Storm

anything that caused me pain. The minute I was distressed, I shut off emotionally.

I felt two emotions: anger and anger. If I had a moment of happiness, it was quickly replaced by anger. Everything pissed me off. I did not become physical with my anger, because I knew the consequences of that, but my anger internalized and created health problems. It was this anger that made me realize that I was no longer going to allow those around me to dictate my happiness. I was not going to allow others to control that fearful part of me. At that point, I did not care what they thought about my condition or me. I was no longer going to live in fear of their perceptions of who they thought I was, or the stigma of PTSD.

I recall sitting in a staff meeting one day. The meeting occurred soon after I was diagnosed. I am not sure what led to the conversation, but PTSD was definitely not part of the general topic. Regardless of the topic of conversation, one of my coworkers began discussing an individual he had previously encountered. He referred to the individual as a *PTSD individual.* Right then, I sat back and realized that my coworker had already made an assumption about PTSD. He had already labeled this individual with the term PTSD. He had based his judgment on the premise that the individual he was referring to appeared to be angry much of the time and was a seasoned military person. I was shocked that my coworker had made that statement. I thought, *It's no wonder why people who are suffering are suffering in silence. Who wants to feel ostracized by their own peers? Who would ever want to let anyone know they are suffering based on ignorant perceptions of PTSD?*

It was many weeks later that I expressed my disapproval for his comment and told him that I was suffering from PTSD. He was more shocked to learn that he would be assisting me with a document based on things I had encountered during my diagnosis process. At that moment after his comment, I made the clear decision that I was not going to hide my diagnosis. I was not going to suffer in silence. I was going to learn everything I could about PTSD, and I was going to do whatever it took to follow through the process to recovery. Whatever it took. Conquering each fear I encountered, one at a time.

At each step of my recovery and therapy, opportunities have come up for unknown reasons. Rather than fighting against them in fear or questioning them, I have seized those opportunities. Some have ignited a passion to do more with them, and, as a result, I started to become my own cheering section. If I had not done that, you would not be reading this book. For many years, I had a fear of completing this book. It was an unknown area for me. I was not an author. For many years, I knew I would write a book. I had even expressed it in a work performance feedback. I had my own ideas of what I would write about, but I never thought this would be one until I was in treatment.

It was not until I realized there was a greater purpose for my circumstances that I was able to "get the whole picture." I had begun the manuscript both in my head and on paper, but I was afraid of actually writing it out in full. I thought, *What if it's no good? What if no one likes it? And what if I sell many copies and become successful? What if, what if, what if?* I was scared, and my fear kept me from taking action. I became fearful of failing at it. I found a bigger purpose than myself for writing the book. That purpose is you.

I write about the fear because it is where I was living on a daily basis. My whole world revolved around fears. Some appeared for no reason, and that is where the symptoms kicked in and panic attacks took over. Once I grasped the concept that I had created those fears to avoid my emotional pain, I focused on working with the fear rather than avoiding it. I cannot say that I don't get fearful; that is part of me being human. I continue to work with it and study it. I have become my own researcher, per se.

I honestly believe that had I not been so committed to getting my life back, I would not have been so focused on figuring myself out. As with everything else in life that we commit to, committing to myself was most important. I had to commit to working at managing my symptoms and changing my thought process. I was willing to do whatever it took to manage my symptoms and to face the fears of remembering the stuff that I really didn't want to remember. Fear controlled me. I had a fear of the past things I had seen, even though they were not part of my present. They were still controlling my future. I now realize that the trigger for my panic attack at the mall was that I was shopping in the same location where my previous treatment sessions had been. Talk about unconscious thoughts. That's how it begins.

When Doc K said we were going to begin exposure therapy, I was mortified. It meant I would be subjected to each trigger that set me into a state of uncontrollable anxiety. Fear. Even his mere mention of future treatment plans would send me into a state of anxiety. My hands would shake, my heart would pound, and I'd start sweating. I often would have difficulty breathing and would say, "I think I am going to pass out." Of course, Doc K would reassure me that I wasn't going to pass out, but when fear controlled my thoughts, what did he know? I found myself pounding my head wondering what the heck was wrong with me. This was all at the mere mention of what was on the agenda for the following week's session. It was scary.

On the evenings before my appointments, I found myself waking up in the middle of the night with anxiety for no apparent reason. While the reason was obvious to Doc K, it was not obvious to me. When I would tell him that I had woken up in a panic attack the evening before, he would say, "Well, you know why that is, don't you?" I would think, *Give me a friggin' break. If I knew what that was, I would be sitting in your chair.*

Again he would explain to me how the brain handles stress unconsciously and would draw a picture so that I would perhaps finally understand. Fear would trigger my body's automatic response to deal with the thoughts of my appointment. Anxiety kicked in to fight off whatever it thought it had to contend with— just as it had learned to do during the initial event. It was a common theme and a common pattern. I could finally connect the pattern to the nightmares before my appointments. I finally understood what was happening when symptoms escalated during stressful situations. I still have the odd nightmare prior to my appointments—and I still may wake up anxious—but now that I am aware of the reason, I am able to settle and refocus my thoughts. I am able to change my thought process. In fact, the truth is that most of this book was written in the wee hours of the morning after I woke up from a nightmare or panic attack. Even as I complete this current edit, it is 5:22 a.m., and I have been awake after a nightmare since 2:30 a.m. I have learned to refocus. Sure, I may be a bit tired today at work, but I have accomplished that much more and I will sleep better tonight. Smile. It's no surprise that the final edits of this book have taken so long.

Fear also controlled me in other ways. When I first began my treatment process, I often thought in advance what excuse I was going to use to either reschedule or not attend my appointment. However, I had made a promise to myself that *no matter what*, I was going to get through this and focus on what was most important about my treatment sessions: *me*.

I realized that my treatment success and responsibility was up to one person—me. By taking care of myself, I was also taking care of my family. When I look back at all those thoughts of wanting to reschedule, I realize they were all based on the fears that I conjured up prior to the appointments. When I finally decided that the fear of attending appointments was going to provide me far less pain than living another day in anger or with anxiety, there was no opposition. I was not fearful of going to the appointment; I was fearful of what I would encounter when I got there, and I had to accept that I needed to face that if I wanted success.

Eye of the Storm

I still recall the day Doc K mentioned that he was going to purchase a bottle of Vicks for our next appointment. You see, during the incident of 1998, we were encouraged to use Vicks in our masks to cover up any odors we might encounter while we were working at the morgue. After 1998, even the thought of Vicks made me hurl. There was not a hope in heck that I was going to have it right under my nose in real time. The mere mention of his plan of attack sent me into one huge panic. My verbal response became almost habit each time he suggested these wild ideas. I would often reply with, "You're an ass." While you may think that is horrible and verbally abusive, I can assure that these words were my way of adding humor into the mix— followed by pounding my head like I was trying to get something out of it. It was my way to deflect and cope.

Around the same time as what I will refer to as *Operation Vicks,* I received my first set of Anthony Robbins audio CDs, *The Ultimate Edge* series. When I signed up and purchased the CDs, I was focused on finding a way to become motivated to exercise and work out. I never thought it would lead to what would happen next.

After listening to a few CDs, I realized they were not motivational; they were *inspirational.* And I will always be grateful for my purchase and for Anthony Robbins's words of wisdom. On the day that *Op Vicks* was to occur, I had

29

already envisioned that I was going to walk into Doc K's office and open the jar of Vicks with no hesitation.

What actually happened was more than that. I was inspired and determined. I walked into Doc K's office and sat down. He took the Vicks out of the cupboard and sat it on the corner of his desk. He opened the box and placed the jar on the desk. I picked up the jar and I opened it. I grabbed a tissue from a box on the table. I then folded the tissue in half—making it resemble a mask—and placed some of the Vicks on the tissue. I then placed the tissue over my nose, taking in each breath of memories that came along with it. Now, I am not saying that I didn't begin to have anxiety and a rush of emotions while recalling specific images—but I committed to the event regardless of what was going to transpire. I was not willing to allow my fear to get in the way of facing the one thing that was causing me emotional and physical pain.

I could have spent weeks dwelling on the Vicks box. I could have spent months sitting with an unopened jar in my hands. I could have spent years worried about what I would have to face once I opened it, but I didn't. I committed to a decision that on that day I was going to make it happen, and I was not going to allow anything or anyone stop me. I was committed to facing any crappy feelings that may have come up as part of the process. I could have canceled my appointment or not even shown up. But I didn't. I was more committed on that day than I had been for the past year and a half in my treatment. I was committed to *me*. I was committed to facing the fear in order to lessen the pain that went along with it.

Healing is a matter of time, but it is sometimes also a matter of opportunity. —**Hippocrates**

BATTEN DOWN THE HATCHES; THE STORM IS ROLLING IN

Many years before being diagnosed with PTSD, I attended mental health treatments for whatever was ailing me. I began eye movement desensitization and reprocessing, or EMDR. While somewhat of an explanation was provided, what I understood from the explanation was probably not exactly what I had heard. I left that appointment believing that I was different. I believed my brain worked in a totally different way from the way anyone else's worked. It is rather humorous when I now recollect. When others asked about the EMDR and why I was receiving it, my explanation was out to lunch. I know we are all different, but *I* was unique. I would explain that my brain did not know how to process traumatic incidents and that I had been born with this problem. EMDR was helping me. I had no idea that my explanation was *my* interpretation of the one I had been given. I didn't realize it was a wrong one.

I think this is the reason I now ask questions and want to know more about PTSD each time I have an appointment. After all, I believe that PTSD can happen to anyone.

I didn't notice emotional or physical changes within me right away. To tell you the truth, I thought most of my symptoms were normal, and I really didn't pay much attention. Although I had a feeling that something was not right, I don't think I was persistent in the fight to figure out what it was. I took for granted and believed it was "all in my head." I mean, that is what I had heard many times when attending our medical facility. So I started believing it.

In the beginning, I had nightmares. My nightmares began fairly soon after I was done working at the morgue. Then I began having flashbacks. This happened in two different ways. I could be going about a normal day's business and then out of the blue I would get a vision of something I had seen from the event. I would begin thinking about it like I was right back in that moment. I started to feel anxious to the point where I would be out of breath, gasping for air, and sometimes thinking I was having a heart attack. I also suffered (and still occasionally suffer) from olfactory flashbacks. The best way I can explain these is that I would smell a scent similar to the one from the morgue, but there would be no physical smell. It appeared without warning. These types of flashbacks created the most fear for me. Anxiety would set in as soon as I had the sensation of a smell. I would freak out. I had no idea what was happening to me. Sadly enough, I hid and secluded myself when these instances happened.

If I had a flashback while I was at work, I would retreat to my office and stay there until the anxiety passed, sometimes even for an hour. Often the flashback would end long before the anxiety. I dealt with the reality of the anxiety. The anxiety symptoms were often so intense that I thought of dying; that is what they felt like. I would calm myself down to the point that I thought I was okay, and my mind would automatically send me back into panic-attack mode.

Other times, I would pick up the phone and call a family member to talk. I am sure my parents thought I was just calling to check in, and I often envision them now seeing my number on the phone, rolling their eyes, and saying, "Guess who it is again." When I call today, I often joke about it; but the truth is, I am very grateful they were there many of the bad days. I often called just to hear a caring voice on the other end of the phone so that I could calm down and take my mind off the issue. I still have flashbacks, but the intensity of the visual ones is less than it was when I began treatment two years ago. The olfactory flashbacks come now and again, but I can usually bring myself down much more quickly today with the relaxation techniques I have learned.

I was also plagued with sleeplessness. Sleeplessness happened much more frequently years ago than it does today, but it still occasionally happens. Like I mentioned earlier, this book would not have been written had it not been for sleepless nights.

For many years, I fell asleep on the couch. I had no ambition to even get changed out of my daily clothes and go to bed. At my worst point, I would come home from work, barely eat—if at all—and then go to sleep. Like clockwork, I would wake faithfully several times a night for no reason. I am sure some of it was because I had gone to sleep so early in the evening, but sometimes it was because of nightmares. I would awaken suddenly, gasping for air, or already in a state of anxiety. If I woke up, sometimes I would be up for hours before getting back to sleep. I was tired in the morning, tired in the afternoon, and some days I found myself returning from work and going to bed right away. I was exhausted all the time.

My motivation to do anything was almost nonexistent, and it became apparent that things were not quite right. Slowly I became more frustrated and angry over the smallest things that once had never bothered me. I was living in a world of black and white with no hints of gray. I had no problem getting angry and no problem in telling people exactly what I thought, regardless of the outcome and with no regard for how I was delivering the message.

My memory also became terrible. I became one of those people who would write a list of things I needed to do and then forget where I put the list. The things I could easily remember now were tasks. As soon as I became overwhelmed, I would forget—even just seconds after. I consider myself to be a multitasker, but I think I took the term to extremes. Even doing dishes, I would remember something I had forgotten earlier. I would then leave the dishes to do what I had forgotten. When I arrived at that location, I might have noticed something out of place and taken it to where it belonged. For example, I would get to the closet and notice it was a mess and then begin sorting the closet. I would find something in the closet that didn't belong, and then I would go to place it in its location. I am sure by now you get the picture. I was my own circus, and the dishes . . .

I often disassociated, and I didn't even realize there was a name for what I was experiencing. I would often feel I was floating—or even out of my body. Sometimes while driving I would say, "Oh my gosh, am I here already? I don't even remember the drive." That became extremely scary, as I would have no recollection of anything before the point that I "woke up." When I got stressed or was experiencing a flashback, I

Jacqueline Buckley, CD, BA

had a difficult time recalling anything in between. Feeling spacey was normal, and I was not on any medications. The minute stress was elevated, I spaced out.

CUMULONIMBUS

I think sometimes when we have strong personalities and are go-getters by nature, we tend to tell ourselves we are doing okay, but deep down we know we are not. But I think we all know that "de-nile is not just a river in Egypt." I finally realized that I was losing my sense of who I was and who I had been in the past. I knew in that moment that if I were going to make changes, I needed to take charge of myself and insist that someone listen.

 Finding a health-care provider who fit my needs was a process in itself. Through all the years that I had seen mental health providers for one reason or another, the hardest part was finding a perfect match. Many providers do a great job in their fields, but that doesn't mean I felt comfortable with them. I can even recall times I would attend our medical facility, express my concerns, and then be told it was *all in my head.* I was frustrated and tired of the rolling eyes that said, *Oh, it's her again.* I lost all faith in the system that was supposed to be there to support me. Very early on in my process, prior to being diagnosed, I had several providers that I just did not feel comfortable with. It wasn't for any particular reasons; if I weren't feeling comfortable enough to trust, then my commitment level for my treatment was not a top priority.

During the last few years of my military career, I had extreme areas of stress: family, work, and health. My husband and I were separated due to an overseas posting. I was in school full time for dental hygiene. I was coping with a family crisis and assisting with the raising of my granddaughter. I was alone in a city with no family support. When I wasn't in school, I was working. I had my share of responsibilities.

When I reached out to my doctor for assistance, he referred me to a mental health practitioner. Again, I completed tests, talked about past issues, and asked for assistance. I spoke of 1998 and the nightmares. I expressed the flashback symptoms, and after reviewing my medical notes, I noticed even mentions regarding possible PTSD. In my opinion, that was where the pencil stopped. In my view and from the experiences, I understood that I was provided treatment for anxiety and depression. Therapists suggested cognitive-based focusing on the current situation, but nothing discussed related specifically to the event of 1998. Even as I look back and recall, I often wonder if I gave the impression that all was great and that the experience of assisting in the morgue environment didn't affect me. After all, if I believed my vulnerability to not being okay would lead to loss of promotion or others' disapproval, why would I admit I was not okay? But eventually, even those who appear to be strong and holding it all together fall and realize they cannot do it all alone.

In 2004 or 2005, I was questioned about my "smell disturbances" and commented to the doctor about the morgue smells. I had even gone to see a neurologist and attended a sleep clinic, all of which has been documented in my health records. No further investigation was completed (in my view) specifically for symptoms related to 1998.

After graduation from dental hygiene school, I was stationed elsewhere. Nothing changed with the previous stressors; in fact, they were worse than before. My husband was still overseas, and I was moving alone to a new area and still dealing with a family crisis. I had no support. I was tired. My health broke yet again. I was expected to attend a course even after numerous requests to remove me from it for health concerns. I was, in my view, guilt tripped into attending. I had even expressed that I would rather wait and attend at a later date than not be able to give the course 100 percent of my entire being. Even against my own better judgment, I attended just to keep my supervisors happy.

Again, I ignored my own ability to say no and take care of myself.

Shortly after returning from the course—and not receiving my qualification, due to my missing a small portion directly related to my health issues—my husband was finally stationed back home. I then expressed my thoughts and feelings and shared that I was not going to stay in the military beyond my fast approaching twenty years.

Without hesitation, my husband began the process of applying for a job outside the military. We were both surprised when his application to a police agency was accepted, and he was slated to attend training. We would be separated again. I would be alone again to deal with symptoms, physical health concerns, and continued family issues. As a result, I requested a compassionate transfer until I could be released from the military.

I followed the protocols of the process and was assigned a social worker to hear my story. I attended a few appointments and began to see a common theme of having to repeat my story over and over regarding why I was requesting the transfer. When I began questioning why I was repeating myself over and over, I believe I was greeted with unprofessional responses that, in my opinion, bordered on bullying.

I recall the day the social worker made a comment regarding the word *trauma*. When I questioned it and asked if there was something indicated on my medical file, he appeared to become agitated and rude. I stated something like, "If there is something on my file, I want to know about it." He made a few comments, and the next thing I knew I was being referred to a psychiatrist.

At this point, I had still not heard anything regarding my request for a transfer. I was waiting for a specific report. Just after being seen by the psychiatrist, I received a call from the social worker requesting that I meet with him to explain my situation. I responded, "But I have already told you that," or something to that effect. I immediately drafted and sent an e-mail to the psychiatrist with a carbon copy to my supervisor requesting that the social worker be removed from my case. I was frustrated at having to constantly repeat my issues to someone who I believed should have been listening. I did not feel comfortable. I felt as though I was being bullied by that particular heath professional based on the perception of demeanor I perceived each time I asserted myself when feeling I was constantly repeating myself about issues that they should have known.

I recall the day I met with the psychiatrist to give me the results of my testing and our discussion. "You have PTSD," he stated. I was mortified. I recall crying uncontrollably. Those words were imprinted in my mind as clear as

43

some of the events of 1998. I remember stating that I was frustrated and that he could not give me back my time—for all the years I suffered with anxiety, for the added stress of the two years prior without family support, and for the decade in between. I could not get any of it back. It hit me hard. I cried for days. The only solace I had during the entire time was knowing that I had a definitive diagnosis. I could finally commit to a treatment based on an accurate diagnosis.

Even in the midst of an accurate diagnosis, I was never transferred, and my husband and I were separated for an additional nine months prior to my release from the military. For nine months, I was once again alone to face my symptoms and initial treatment. I felt lost. Even the supervisors—who had stood by me when shit hit the fan—became strangers. It was in that moment that I decided to ask for a transfer out of my unit until my final release date. I needed support, and the only support I could rely on was with a unit designed to accommodate those who were unable to work in their normal locations due to illness or injury.

Shortly after the issues regarding the social worker, I decided to file a redress of grievance. It focused on issues surrounding my medical issues, lack of empathy and, in my view, lack of professional treatment. Almost four years after that initial filing, I finally received a response. All requests were denied. I could elaborate on

Eye of the Storm

the outcome, but I have since come to learn that sometimes we have to choose our battles—or at least focus on the battle rather than the defeat.

I learned from that experience that commitment to oneself is critical. If I had not questioned comments or fought for what was not being said, I would have not received my diagnosis—regardless of how painful those words were to hear. I was not without my fault during all those years. I should have spoken up regardless of the outcomes. Even tonight as I once again edit this book, I have learned that two Canadian soldiers who served in Afghanistan have taken their own lives. The news noted that PTSD was a possible factor and that both were changed upon their return. I immediately became frustrated and angry—one apparently suffering in silence. It was such a tragedy, and in addition to thoughts for those families came another thought. A quote from a great leader, the late General Norman Schwarzkopf, goes like this: "No organization will ever get better until they realize something is wrong."

There was nothing wrong with my standing up for and expressing what was not working. However, in order to really appreciate if something was not working, I needed to give it my undivided attention. I needed to be committed to the task. What I finally learned from the whole process was that I was responsible

45

for my own health and well-being. If I didn't get the results or answers from a health-care professional that made me feel safe and assured, then I had to be persistent. There is an old saying: *The squeaky wheel is the one that gets oiled.* I became the squeaky wheel, and I am sure someone remembers me as being a pain in the ass. But I got the results I needed, and I also committed to those results—and to myself. I didn't complain and insist on change or help and then do nothing about it when it was provided.

In my struggle to find a health-care provider who would not only *listen* but also take the time to figure this thing out, I was committed to the task. I didn't have the energy, and at times I felt I was getting nowhere—but I was committed. My commitment and persistence is what got me the help I was searching for. I wanted change and problems solved overnight. I wanted the job done. I believed that because it was a priority to me, it should have been everyone else's. I ran into obstacles and struggles mainly when dealing with outside agencies working on my military file. I could write a whole other book about my frustrations in this area, but the fact is that I was getting frustrated about things I could not control. I decided to shift my frustration and recognized that I could no longer accept the ignorance of others as my excuse for slipping back into old behaviors. I looked for a solution and followed through. I became resourceful and accountable. I can tell you this is not an easy thing to learn when you are living with anger, hurt, resentment, sadness, or frustration. I know one of the biggest lessons I learned was that I needed to ground myself and get myself into check before I dealt with others on the phone or in person. I had to stop making things *personal* even though they were to me.

Forgiving does not erase a bitter past. A healed memory is not a deleted memory. Instead, forgiving what we cannot forget creates a new way to remember. We can change the memory of our past into a hope for the future.—**Lewis B. Smedes**

EXPOSED TO THE ELEMENTS

I mentioned memory and dissociation earlier. It was explained to me that often when we are faced with tragic events, our minds find a place where they can cope. I don't quite understand this natural survival mechanism, but over a three-year process, I have learned about it in a way that makes sense. Doc K explained that sometimes an event—as we remember it—is broken in sequence. Like a movie reel with thousands of frames, sometimes those frames are erased. There are missing links. Bit by bit I would work at trying to put the movie back together.

Doc K has been someone I have grown to trust. He has always taken time to explain things to me in such a way that I have been able to understand. It is through that understanding that I have been able to process my emotions and analyze myself. I am able to understand my triggers, understand how to calm myself down much more rapidly, and—most importantly—I now understand that I am going to be okay.

I had never done exposure therapy in the past. In fact, I don't recall anything I had ever accomplished in therapy as successful as exposure. While it has been emotionally painful and tiring, I have learned more about myself. I have a greater understanding of how the traumatic event has affected my life. Some people I have spoken with think that exposure therapy is not a good choice for treatment for PTSD. They believe that constantly introducing the trauma only brings up more trauma. I would argue and say that it is healthy to face fears that have paralyzed us emotionally. I know the exposure experiences have allowed me to come to terms emotionally with what I have gone through. These exposure portions have all been done in a therapeutic setting. If I had dwelled on the unhappiness of the event and constantly discussed it without making a connection emotionally, then it would have led to an unproductive way of thinking. Now, when (or if) I have a flashback, I can associate the meaning of that flashback, rather than disassociating from it or pretending that the event did not happen.

My exposure has been combined with EMDR, eye movement desensitization and reprocessing. It can be done in several ways, but I have had most of my EMDR with a light bar. As I recalled certain events, my eyes followed a light back and forth; this allowed me to process the thought. The light continued and then stopped. During my sessions, after the light stopped I was asked to talk about my thoughts and whatever came to mind next. As I shared and then finished talking, I would again refocus on the light. The process was repeated. The goal was to retrieve the memories I had previously lost or forgotten—another piece of my memory movie reel.

Areas of my memory were distorted and missing. I would get so frustrated to the point that I would cry. I have seen movies in which someone has amnesia, but I never really understood that until I experienced the feeling for myself. The memory is not there. No matter how hard I tried to recall a specific detail or time, it was not there. I often questioned myself during sessions as to whether I had even been part of the team working at the hangar. To this day, there are still things I cannot recall. I continue to work on remembering, but I no longer beat myself up over *not* remembering. I understand now that I am not crazy (as I often thought) and that this is all a normal process.

Remembering has been difficult emotionally, but I have grown more in the past two and a half years than I have done in a lifetime. I have become more compassionate, and grateful, and I have become much more patient than I was during the eleven years of living with PTSD and being unsure of what was wrong with me.

One short, pivotal memory I have that I am very fond of happened during our deployment to the hangar. During a shift, I took a few minutes to sit down. I sat on the stairs of our dental van. Not long after I sat down, Charlie joined me. We began chatting. I am pretty sure my reason for sitting had something to do with a task I had been given with a torso, and I was reflecting and trying to cope. It made me think. My memory in this area is still missing some links, but I do somewhat recall the conversation, and I may have even shed a tear. I stated that I realized that life was very short and that we should be grateful for each day that is given to us. I continued talking about never letting the day end with anger toward those we love. My mind was fixated on wondering if each person aboard that flight had taken the chance to let someone close to them know that they were loved. I wondered if they knew that someone loved them. Once again, I wondered if that man had spoken to his family before leaving on that flight. From one specific task, my mind began to race and think. I was overwhelmed with deep sadness, frustration, anger, and resentment. My mind raced for answers, but I could not find any.

For much of my time at that hangar, the remains I encountered were small. For that one task, however, I witnessed more; I could not comprehend or even begin to cope. I felt as though it was all part of a movie. It has been determined through recall that this moment, this specific event—this piece in time—was my trigger. While memories are still imprinted, the meaning of those memories has changed. I owe that change to being able to talk about each issue as if it were yesterday. I was able to connect my emotions and talk, cry, or be angry; I could put meaning to things I had no idea had any connection.

Small things came to light as I recalled and made connections. For example, I came home at the end of each shift. Until this year, I could not remember what my bathroom looked like. I could not recall where the tub, shower, or toilet sat in the bathroom's floor plan. This was a place I had chosen to forget, as it symbolized pain. After a few sessions of trying to remember, I decided to do an Internet search for our military married quarters floor plans, just so that I could close that chapter and understand it. I found my answer and understood it. For many years after 1998—without understanding the connection—anytime I was in emotional pain, I would retreat to the shower or take a bath. My tears could never be found in the water; they just washed down the drain. As an ironic twist, my ideas about this book flowed while I was in the shower. I would either have to jump out of the shower to write things down immediately, or struggle to recall when I was done.

For many years, I would not sleep in my bed; I slept on the couch. During exposure, I realized that my connection to my bedroom was also the connection to that night. The evening of the tragic event, I had been awakened from sleep. I associated what had once been a restful place to a place of pain—and found it difficult to sleep in my bedroom for that reason. This became worse as the years progressed, and my physical body suffered because of it. I had no idea why I could not sleep in my bed until I found the connection. Now that I understand, I enjoy a restful sleep in my bed. I honestly believe that if I had not embraced exposure therapy, I would still be trying to figure things out today, and I would still be miserable. For that I am grateful.

Whatever forms of meditation you practice, the most important point is to apply mindfulness continuously, and make a sustained effort. It is unrealistic to expect results from meditation within a short period of time. What is required is continuous sustained effort.—**Dalai Lama**

EYE OF THE STORM

The art of mindfulness has been an essential part of my healing. As with commitment, you are the only one who can participate in mindfulness; no one else can do it for you. It has been a vital part of my process.

I was first introduced to mindfulness many years ago. I was not only introduced to mindfulness, but also introduced to understanding my feelings and where they originate within my body. From my interpretation and understanding, mindfulness is being present in the present moment. It is training yourself to be aware of your surroundings as you view them. It involves opening up all your senses to take in what surrounds you, even if that's just one thing, such as listening to all the sounds that occur around you as they happen. It is also my understanding that when we are in a state of mindfulness, we cannot be in a state of PTSD, because PTSD is an unconscious state that keeps us disassociated. When we are mindful, we are fully aware. The other cannot live.

Eye of the Storm

In the beginning, I found it really difficult to concentrate and take even five minutes for myself to be still and think. I was a doer. I was always on the go. A perfectionist, I was always planning the next thought before the last had finished. I would be naive to think that I am the only person who suffers from this trait. The great news was that I was able to tone it down a bit. Well, long enough to take time to meditate or just be mindful. Today, I often stay in bed in the morning. I'm fully awake, and I stop my mind from racing. Sometimes I just listen to the sounds around me, or I place myself into deep relaxation.

I often use the mindfulness strategy when I am hit by a wave of anxiety; it helps me change my thought process in order to get my breathing under control and bring my symptoms down faster. This helps me by not allowing the symptoms to escalate to a peak state. For example, one afternoon I was driving alone when a plane flew overhead. In the past, this has sent my anxiety to a ten in a fraction of a second. Once I became mindful of my emotions and thoughts, I would say things to myself like, *The grass is green, the car in front of me is white, my hands are warm, and the sun is warm on my face.* It may sound bizarre, but this would break my thought process and have me focusing on the moment rather than the what-ifs that started to consume my mind after I saw the plane. I began using this technique when my anxiety seemed out of control, even during treatment. The only difference was I would not say those things out loud; instead, I would focus more on my breathing and each breath I took in and out. I would focus on feeling the air entering my nostrils and listening to the sound of my breath as I exhaled out of my mouth.

Focusing on the *now* means we cannot focus on the future or the past. You are in the moment, and that is the moment of the present. If we are not focusing on the past, then we are not remembering the past; nor are we stuck in it. If we are not focused on the future, then we are not allowing ourselves to think about things that have not happened; we can't worry about anything in the future. Mindfulness has helped me tremendously, and while it seems like a simple concept, it takes practice. Each time you think of something other than what is in the moment, you are not being mindful. This is what happened many times when I would disassociate during my treatment. Things would become so overwhelming and painful to remember that I would begin thinking of other things—or not think of anything at all. I would be in what I called *la-la land*. When I wasn't being mindful of what was going on, I often could not even focus or hear someone talking to me. I was zoned out.

It was only when I began really practicing my mindfulness techniques that I could keep myself from veering off into la-la land for more than a few minutes. Now if I disassociate from the present, I don't do it for as long as I did before. I am in the moment. I am not thinking about the what-ifs of the future, and I am not thinking about being stuck in the past. I am here, present in what is going on right now. When I do begin wandering off into my future or past states, I am quickly able to bring myself back to a normal state (seeing as I joke and say that I am not normal to begin with). This happens within a few moments rather than the eternity that it felt like in the past to those who were around me. What used to take fifteen or twenty minutes now takes less than five. I am happy with that, and the more I practice being mindful, the more I can work on getting that timing under a minute. I know things might always come up that trigger memories, but as long as I can recognize them as soon as possible—and get a handle on my emotions and become mindful—I am not fearful.

I think the biggest issue for those of us who suffer from PTSD is the feeling of being uncertain and fearful of the unknown. I was always worried that I would just cry for no apparent reason or have a panic attack in public. I worried about what others would think. But the truth is that I am not so worried about those things anymore. I will face them and deal with them when they happen. PTSD can keep us from the normal things we enjoy. It's the fear of the storm that keeps us from enjoying jumping in the puddles. I disliked crowds and often avoided certain activities because I worried, *What if I have a panic attack or flashback?* But I was not being mindful. Once I stopped worrying about the issue and placed myself in the present moment, I was able to handle the situation more confidently.

I am not a religious person. I have my beliefs and an appreciation for religions, but I don't practice any particular one. I consider myself a spiritual being. Regardless of my beliefs in this area, I accept that we all need to find something to focus on in order to find our inner peace. Regardless of what it is—yoga, meditation, prayer, or mindfulness—they all fall into the eye of the storm, our zone of inner peace. I chose to take a mixture of different traditions and have applied them to my own life. It is my way of grounding myself and finding my inner peace—a place I go, to be in the moment. Some people find it in nature; some find it practicing yoga or meditation. When I began my therapy sessions, I was a *"donkey on the edge"*. I was very high-strung and didn't know how to relax. My body was in hyper mode all the time. Butterflies lived in my stomach on a constant basis; I was anxious at a lower level 24-7. My body knew no other feeling. My resting heart rate used to be from the high 70s to 80s. I am happy to share that it is now low to mid-60s. What changed? My ability to relax in the calm. In the eye. Focusing on things that I can control, not things I can't.

I began downloading hypnosis applications on my iPad, and I began using them each night in order to relax and fall asleep. After repetitive use, I could just lie down and relax without the recordings. I could—and still do—place my body in a state of total relaxation. I don't feel the butterflies in my belly, and I am aware of my slow, deliberate breathing.

I also began being grateful for things on a daily basis. In the beginning, I would mentally take note of at least one thing each day I was grateful for. Now, I have found an application for tracking gratitude, and it allows me to express it while recording it in the app. Being grateful for things has allowed me to become open to the small things around me that I may have taken for granted in the past. It allows me to appreciate the people and things around me. It has also given me another reason to think beyond my own despair and pain. When I am grateful for something, I cannot be angry or sad about things in the past—or be anxious about the future. I am grateful in the moment.

When I made the decision for my book, I became overwhelmed with thinking about the past and the future. I was worried that I would not have much to say; most of it was in my head in the many speeches I had given in my mind. Once I became mindful and stayed in my present, I realized that the words flowed onto the page as if I were speaking them out loud in a speech. I have come to realize that worrying about the future or living in the past keeps us from truly enjoying the beauty of things around us. It paralyzes our minds in such a way that we become stuck in the pain of whatever we have decided that is; it's like we enjoy being there because it's what seems to be most comfortable. Just remember, if you're mindful, you can't be focusing on the past or the future—just the here and now. You're in the eye of the storm.

YESTERDAY, TODAY, AND TOMORROW

There are two days in every week about which we should not worry—two days which should be kept free of fear and apprehension.

One of these days is yesterday with its mistakes and care, its faults and blunders. All the money in the world cannot bring back yesterday.

The other day we should not worry about is tomorrow with its possible adversities, its burdens, its large promise and poor performance. Tomorrow also is beyond our immediate control. Tomorrow's sun will rise either in splendor or behind a mask of clouds—but it will rise. Until it does, we have no stake in tomorrow, for it is as yet unborn.

That leaves only one day—today. Anyone can fight the battles of just one day. It is only when you and I add the burdens of those two awful eternities—yesterday and tomorrow—that we break down.

It is not the experience of today that drives us mad—it is remorse or bitterness for something that happened yesterday, and the dread of what tomorrow may bring. Let us, therefore, journey but one day at a time.

—Author unknown

The above poem was given to me by my mother in April 1998. She passed away in July of that year. Perhaps her intuition and spiritual guidance had spoken to her. Perhaps somehow she knew—through forces of which I can only assume—that I would need a reminder at some point in the years to follow. I have carried this poem with me since. And although I have shared this poem with others, it has been within the past three years that I have gotten a true understanding of its meaning.

Through humor, you can soften some of the worst blows that life delivers. And once you find laughter, no matter how painful your situation might be, you can survive it.—**Bill Cosby**

PUDDLES AND MUD

We have all heard the expression *laughter is the best medicine*. When we are laughing, we are not only present in the moment, but we are also releasing endorphins,[2] which are our bodies' own natural chemical that produces an opiate effect. In today's society with the drug problem that exists, if we all understood the power of laughter, perhaps we would not have so many people dependent on manmade chemicals that break us down. Dr. Norman Cousins laughed his way back to health by entertaining himself with funny shows and laughing. When we are laughing, we are not crying about the past or worrying about the future.

Finding humor when I suffered from depression was challenging at first, but it is another critical area that helped me—and still helps me—cope and manage today. When I was feeling miserable, the last thing I wanted to do

---

[2] spb.royalsocietypublishing.org
Article: Social laughter is correlated with elevated pain threshold

was to be joyous and happy. Being miserable was what I was about. If I could find a way, that is what I made happen. The *M* in my middle name stood for "miserable," not "Marie."

I have no idea when I realized I had lost my sense of humor, but something finally hit me and I found it again. Perhaps it was when, as a result of both our jobs, I was separated from my husband, who was in Belgium—leaving us apart for two and a half years. Or dealing with an ill family member who had an addiction issue. Or perhaps dealing with a supervisor on a daily basis whose level of compassion could be compared to that of a crow pecking at a wounded animal. I mean, seriously, all that crap had to have been a joke, right? How the heck does one person handle everything without a sense of humor?

Throw life into the mix of PTSD and all its symptoms; I needed to find some humor. Laughing at my circumstances was much easier than facing how I often really felt. I mean, I couldn't go about my day throwing dishes at the wall. Well, I suppose I could have, but that's not the point. I made a decision to really work on finding something lighthearted within the things that were tough.

Getting frustrated has—and still is—an easy place for me to go when I am overwhelmed in a situation. If I stay focused on the present, I am often able to find some sort of humor in a given situation, or I at least try to find optimism in it by perhaps giving it a different view. It certainly takes practice, but I worked hard at finding a way to laugh at the things that otherwise made me nuts with frustration, or things that made me angry. Now I don't work on it as hard; it's become a habit and a new way of life. My husband often calls me a dork because sometimes in the midst of serious being, I have no problem jumping in puddles or playing in the mud.

When my husband and I met, we found commonalities that kept the kid in us alive. We loved to watch the *Scooby-Doo* movies; even today, we both laugh when I do my Scooby impression. I also owe a huge thanks to my friend Kelly and her husband for introducing me to *The Big Bang Theory*. It does not matter how many times I watch an episode, I still laugh. When I sit down to watch TV, I enjoy watching shows that will either inspire me or make me laugh. The news is not on my list of favorite channels, and only on occasion do we watch it.

While I am driving to work, I would rather listen to the comedy network or comedy channels than listen to the same music repetitively. I look for opportunities to smile and laugh, even if I am laughing at myself. Being able to laugh at ourselves and our mistakes is what keeps us from beating ourselves up for days and ending up in a deeper depression. It's about laughing at the small things that really will not make a difference tomorrow. It's a much better option than the frustration or anger that entices us to take it out on others by saying things we don't mean. When I was pissed off, I was pissed off. No one could take that away from me. *Grrrr, I am angry because you left the milk out on the counter and you are going to know about it!* Often what I was angry about were things I could not control, or things that were out of my control.

To laugh and find the humor in things, I had to be mindful (there's that word again). I had to be mindful enough to distinguish between the things that I could control and the things I couldn't. I had to stop taking things personally. As the old saying goes, *don't sweat the small stuff.* Getting angry was easy. It didn't take long for me to go from a zero to a ten on the frustration scale when a minor mishap occurred, but once I was able to let go of the control factor, I could take those certain instances and laugh at them.

In the midst of driving, I had to learn to appreciate and laugh at the car in front of me if the driver made an error. Better yet, I had to own *my* driving errors, and rather than ignore the person giving me the finger, I would smile and make the silly *oops, I am sorry* look. Rather than start a full-blown road rage, I would smile, change my face, and in my head say, *Nice blinker, asshole.* Those words alone in a calm tone to myself were enough to make me laugh out loud. And the laughing was at myself for using the potty word rather than at the incident itself.

Another example happened one afternoon while putting together some furniture while my husband was at work. I had previously forgotten to put away a kit of different screws, bolts, and washers. I had left the box on the counter. As I passed by the counter with the kitchen chair I had just proudly assembled on my own, I knocked the edge of the container—sending the whole thing across the floor. It opened and hailed more than a few hundred small pieces along with it. My initial response was "Ahhh, *shit*," which was followed by a chuckle as I looked into the container and noticed that only three little pieces had not made it with their fellow mates on the floor. I sat on the floor and stared in awe. *I am such a dork*, I thought, chuckling. I was truly stunned that all the little bits were on the floor, but I was also laughing that only three were left in the box. After I scooped them all up and put them into a Ziplock bag, I reflected back on how I might have reacted had that incident happened just two years prior. I know I would have flung that container, making sure that the last three pieces made it on the floor with the rest of the pile. I would have kicked the container and spread the mess over the floor, all just to prove a point. I would have been upset for hours, cried about it, and would have spent at least two or three hours separating each piece in order to return it to its proper location. The chaos would have been too much to bear with them being out of place, or I would have scooped them all up in a dustpan and thrown everything into the garbage.

I believe that to find humor in challenges, it is essential to relax, breathe, and just be. Laughing at myself was far better than being critical of what I'd done. I could do *critical* quite well all on my own. I learned to internalize everything personally. I learned to cope with stress the best way I knew how, and I disassociated from any memory or situation that caused me pain. I am not saying that in *all* challenging or unexpected situations I found—or needed to find—something funny, and trust me, I often didn't. But now when I take a time-out during a situation, I can look at it from a different perspective and sometimes find humor in the smallest part of the situation. I needed to laugh, relax, and just be. I had learned soon after the incident of 1998 to do my best to control everything in order to avoid pain, but by controlling, I was actually *out* of control. I have found the humor in my own ditzy moments, rather than get upset over little things or things that are not within my control.

I recall one therapy session with Doc K when I was telling him of a work situation that had me all riled up. I now realize that I am candid in my storytelling, but on that day—as I was discussing my frustration—Doc K stopped me and said, "When you discuss this at work, you're going to do it without the head bob, right?" His comment stopped me right in my tracks. And I began visualizing the side-to-side attitude head weaving that he had just said I had done. I had no idea that when I was telling a story—especially one where *self* was being threatened or attacked—that I did it in such a candid way. I began to laugh, and in that moment, the stress in my body faded. I was calm. I was even calm when I continued to tell the story. Finding humor and laughter is so important. Now it's like air, and I could not imagine life without it. Take time to laugh and enjoy the small things.

Life is hard. Then you die. Then they throw dirt in your face. Then the worms eat you. Be grateful that it happens in that order.—**David Gerrold**

SMALL VICTORIES: MY LIFE JACKET FOR MANAGING CHAOS

Sometimes when we have breakthrough accomplishments, we celebrate—especially if the accomplishments are huge. However, in my quest to be a working superhero, I often became overwhelmed with the quantity of tasks, regardless of the magnitude. I never slowed down, and I could never let anyone see me as anyone other than an emotionally strong individual. I wanted to be perceived as someone who could be counted on to get the job done, regardless of the sacrifices. But, like any superhero, I had my weakness, my own breaking point or nemesis that could take me down without warning. I am human. That concept alone made me vulnerable to mental and physical exertion, along with a vast array of emotional turmoil. My superhero force field eventually began to break down.

While tornados are measured on a Fujita scale and hurricanes as categories, I measured myself on the *eggshell scale*. In fact, I recall one of my coworkers stating that she never knew from one day to the next what type of mood I would be in when I came into work. She said she "walked on eggshells," not wanting to upset me. While her analogy assisted me in making changes, it reflected her perception of what I was feeling.

When I was working, I was not the type of person who would get uncontrollably angry or go on a rampage toward those I was supervising. But I can only imagine that my body language and facial expressions showed more than I was willing to share verbally. My internal storm was so intense that getting out of bed or combing my hair was a huge task. While I am grateful that I never steered down the path, I could have easily allowed myself to get caught up in an addiction. I could have made that my present, the focus of my day—rather than taking care of myself or others. My to-do list was endless, and it always appeared that it was getting bigger. My motivation and ability to accomplish anything on it was falling, however.

I had always been a go-getter. I was organized and would swim rather than sink. When I was given a task—even if I didn't have a clue how I was going to accomplish it—I took on the adventure. I was a fighter, but for some reason I was now sinking and had no ambition or drive to do anything. I was not interested in taking on one more job, or even dealing with one more issue at home. I was adapting the attitude of *I don't care*, and it was approaching fast and furious. I was spiraling into a storm and spitting out the anger and frustration as a result. If someone approached me at work with another task, I had no problem letting them know how I was feeling. Usually it came out with me becoming frustrated and overwhelmed.

I even recall the day my boss added another item to my to-do list. I remember my reaction to his request. I shut the door and replied, "I am done." I had no problem letting him know that he needed to delegate out my endless list because I was sick and tired of being called upon to complete what I felt was everyone else's job. I hated the feeling. It was not me. I was born to succeed, but the only thing I was succeeding at was being bitter. Bitterness had no personal attachment to any specific person or task. It just was what it was. All I knew is that I didn't like who I was, or why I was becoming more angry and resentful. Although I was seeing someone for the issues in my life, and to learn coping strategies, I had no idea how or what to do to at least gain some leverage in my ability to get through the day.

Along the way, I was introduced to the Operational Stress Injury Social Support (OSISS) group coordinator. He invited me to a group meeting. At that point, I had no idea that anyone besides me was suffering with PTSD. I chuckle about that now, but at the time it was a very real thought. When I walked into the room, I was surprised that I was not the only one there. I was also very scared and nervous. He asked us all to introduce ourselves and say a bit about ourselves. I don't recall much about what I said; I am quite sure the stress had kicked in and I zoned out into my *la-la land*. But I must have complained about my to-do list and not being motivated because I heard a voice pipe up and say "Small victories."

I looked up and listened as Karl explained what he meant. Now, I am sure I didn't hear everything he said. My focus was not there, but I heard enough to take the words literally and apply them to my situation. The concept of *small victories* changed the way I looked at life. It still helps me today, and I have shared it with many. It is a very simple concept but one that I believe is valuable both in healing and in life in general. How could such a simple concept make a huge impact for the better? By adapting this concept, I was able to minimize my frustration and anger in a huge way—especially where my to-do list was involved. I even believe that if we teach our children this concept, we can teach them to celebrate everything they do in general. Perhaps kids would not grow up believing they have to accomplish great things in order to make their parents proud. This concept taught me that

I could be proud of each moment, not just the pop flies.

My PTSD symptoms were so intense that they would often leave me physically drained with absolutely zero motivation. I became overwhelmed before becoming overwhelmed. I awoke in the morning and began thinking of each and every accomplishment that I believed I had to accomplish that day. It overwhelmed me and I hadn't even gotten out of bed yet. When I shifted my thoughts to the *small victories* concept, I was able to celebrate each small task rather than feeling as if I had failed for each one that I had not completed. I allowed myself the choice to accept that if it did not get everything accomplished, it was okay. It didn't mean I was less of a go-getter. It meant that I needed to stop, breathe, and allow myself time for me. As the old saying goes, *I took time to smell the roses*.

My mind was often clouded with unnecessary negative chatter. I was always thinking, thinking and thinking. My mind never shut off. Now when that occurs, I meditate. I become mindful and take time to just *be*. I relax and take a moment to focus on a quiet space.

It is ironic that in the midst of trying to control everything around me, I also wanted to be an overachiever. It seemed bizarre when I thought about it, but today I can relate to it and understand. I could not control my world around the emotions and turmoil I was feeling surrounding the event, so I worked hard at trying to control everything around me. The problem with that concept was that the more we try to control things that aren't in our control, the more we fall apart. The angrier we become. The more I focused on achieving and controlling, the more I allowed others to manipulate and influence me. This occurred in all aspects of my life, but mostly at work. I didn't want to stir the pot, so I complied with everything that was said and done. However, the only pot I was stirring was my own. It was filled with anger and frustration.

I made it considerably easy for others to think I was emotionally strong. In fact, I heard that comment a lot. I was tired of hearing it. I had created my own imitation world of being strong. For many years, I complied and got the job done. I built that perception so that I didn't have to face the most important issue, the truth: the horrific and terrible truth of what I witnessed, the truth that I was not feeling okay emotionally or physically, the truth that I didn't have all the answers, and the truth that I hated getting up in the morning. Most importantly, I didn't want to face the truth that I just wanted the memories to go away as if nothing had ever happened.

Even the response given in a social work report with regards to my contingency/compassionate request appeared to minimize the magnitude of my situation. "Many individuals in the CF are afflicted with PTSD" was my social worker's response. While I could agree that this may have been the case, I wondered how many were dealing with those two issues at the same time. "Her situation is neither unique nor exceptional," they said. It both frustrated and boggled my mind that my situation wasn't considered unique. I was dealing with severe PTSD, no family support, separation from my spouse due to employment, and dealing with a family member who was ill with an addiction. I was fighting a losing battle and had to find another way to cope, get support, and ride out the waves. I am so thankful for the OSISS peer support group and Karl's advice.

Using the small victories concept became more about my praising myself for each accomplishment individually, rather than looking at the whole picture and wondering how I would ever get through it. But I got through it, I weathered the storm of the bullshit around me, rode out the waves of frustration, and climbed aboard the life raft of peer support. I also gave myself permission to just be myself. In my world, it was very rare to have someone let you know you were doing a great job, or for someone to thank you for taking the time to do something above and beyond your normal daily routine. I learned that if I was not going to be my own cheerleader, no one was. Today, if someone says, "Thanks for doing that, you're awesome,"

Jacqueline Buckley, CD, BA

I reply, "Yeah, I know," with a smile and chuckle. Sure, it feels great to get a compliment for doing a great job at something, but it's even greater knowing yourself that *you are awesome*.

Even today when I attend my appointments with Doc K, he often reminds me of the accomplishments and struggles I have overcome. I can't seem to recall—or maybe I don't weigh my accomplishments in the same magnitude that I used to. Each accomplishment is just that, a small victory.

I hate the giving of the hand unless the whole man accompanies it.—**Ralph Waldo Emerson**

AT THE END OF
THE RAINBOW

Other than with my husband, my dearest friend Kelly, and of course the support group, I had not shared a whole bunch about anything I was dealing with. Even today I gauge what I share and what I don't. If it can help support and inspire others, I tend to share. If it has no reasonable or logical meaning, I don't.

My husband knew I was not feeling well. He knew I could go from calm to angry in a split second, but he had no idea why. As I look back over those years, I truly understand why I never bothered with relationships or even wanted to work on them. I had zero tolerance for ignorance or disrespect. I guess today I still share that concept, but the difference is I am able to let it go—most of the time. I channel my frustrations into constructive resolutions rather than being constantly angry. I have learned that I am as individual as the next person and that I have the right to decide which storms I will chase and which ones I won't.

Only since my husband and I have been together have I been able to share my thoughts, emotions, and struggles without being labeled. I am thankful that he is my opposite. While we have similarities, we also balance what each of us lacks. Sharing my diagnosis and treatment and explaining things to him was easy, but it was not so easy in the beginning to share with my children, or with others.

I found support and needed to allow those around me the opportunity to try to understand what I was going through. I realized that I was not the only person who was affected by my PTSD. They were just as affected as I was. They were the recipients of my anger, my seclusion, and sometimes my lack of compassion. As I look back over the years at how I was emotionally unavailable for my children, I can only look back as a lesson and understand the true magnitude of how it affected them over the years. And yes, it has affected them. For many years I was not capable of emotionally connecting with them. As they got older, it became much easier to let them be independent. It was emotionally easier at the time.

Through understanding all that goes along with PTSD, I have also had to come to terms with the fact that using it as an excuse was neither constructive nor productive in my recovery process. I know I have made mistakes, but I have learned that I cannot allow those mistakes to send me into a world of guilt.

A year or so ago, my daughter expressed that I had not been there emotionally for her. It was a tough revelation to accept, but while I was able to accept her truths, I was also able to express that I would not allow it to make me feel guilty for the rest of my life. I admitted that I had not been there emotionally for many years—and that I was sorry for that. I was not perfect. I could only work at being emotionally there from that point on. As I had stated in the doctor's office the day I was diagnosed: "You cannot give me back my time for all the lost years of going undiagnosed." So the time lost could not be given back to *her*. She could remain angry at me for the rest of my life, or we could both accept that it was done and that "it, too, would pass." It was a day filled with both tears of sadness and tears of joy.

My husband has been one of my biggest supporters, and I can say that we have had our share of marital bliss and blahs. It's funny how the longer you are with someone, the more you tend to miss the small stuff that makes that person the special person he or she is. My husband and I talk all the time. We have always been best friends. We laugh and have arguments like everyone else. In the midst of my treatments, I became somewhat numb to everything—even more than when my symptoms were at their peak. Just as a reminder for things

Eye of the Storm

I may not have been able to see, Doc K was there to remind me once again about how great my hubby was. I had forgotten the small stuff: for every appointment—and sometimes there were two a week—he not only drove me there, but also sat and waited and then drove me home. He held my hand as we walked in and he was there to hold my hand as we walked out. He allowed me the silence I needed on the drive home or listened as I shared my session. He has been by my side, and for that I am thankful each day. In the midst of it all, I needed that little reminder.

If I were not able to share my situation with my family, I would not have been able to accept their support and understanding. I have met many of my peers who are suffering, and there have been break-ups. I have often wondered if there had been support for the family—or at least an understanding of what they were dealing with—would things have been different for them?

When I was first diagnosed, I asked about support groups in the area. As I mentioned earlier, I became connected to one. It was a great starting point for me. I think if I had not been so tenacious about finding resources, I wouldn't have found or had been willing to accept the support on any level. I realized that alone, I was not enough to get me through the tough times.

In the beginning, while I never really had any issues in communicating, I was not always willing to communicate. I kept things to myself until the silence got so unbearable that I felt I was going to burst. That is when I went to see a counselor. If I had taken the time to share what I was bearing with my family or friends, perhaps they would have understood the circumstances of my life better. Commit to working each day at learning to communicate on a more open level.

It is better to conquer yourself than to win a thousand battles. Then the victory is yours. It cannot be taken from you, not by angels or by demons, heaven or hell.—**Buddha**

A NEW DAY

We all know we cannot control a storm, but what we *can* control is how we prepare, react, and ride it out. Giving up control was a huge request in my world. Giving up control meant leaving myself vulnerable to my emotions—and even more—to the unknown. But the truth is, giving up control was my gateway to healing.

For the past two and a half years, I have gone to my appointments at Doc K's. Each week I enter the office, sit down, and work at recalling the events as I remember them. I have been scared in the process and even gotten angry and cried, but not once have I gotten up in the middle of a session and left because I wanted to control the outcome. Many times while recalling, I have had a full-blown, can't-breathe, and feel-like-I-am-going-to-pass-out panic attack. Many times I have been so angry that I wanted to just throw something at the wall. However, with a tissue as the only thing in my hand during appointments, I know that would not have gone well. The point is that my high state of emotions has not dictated my need to control and shut down my healing. I have been there to ride out the storm.

In the past, when I was faced with highly stressful situations or even emotional turmoil, my unconscious brain kicked in. I would either disassociate from what was happening so that I could cope, or I would alter the plan on my own by altering the outcome—by controlling it. For instance, if I were worried about a doctor's appointment or afraid of a procedure, I would either not show up, cancel, or go but make up some excuse as to why I could not have something done that day—and then I'd leave the appointment feeling better. I controlled the appointment to avoid the pain of having to face whatever emotional pain the appointment may have caused.

For many of the earlier years, I tried to control my relationships by staying in them, even though I knew they were not for me. If I controlled them and tried to fix them, I didn't have to face any emotional pain of being alone and having to fix myself. If I were dealing with everyone and everything else around me, trying to always control and fix situations, I wouldn't have to think about the emotional pain that I was living with.

I am not sure when I began realizing that I was making a shift in my behavior and starting to consciously let go of the things I could not control, but the point is, I *did*. I finally realized that there were things I could control and things I could not, and as long as I could recognize those I *couldn't* control—and just let go and let be—I was making progress.

Several times during my therapy sessions, I would be trying to remember something. I would get so frustrated, I would pound on my head trying to control my thoughts and force them to think and remember. I could remember certain things about the morgue, about people I worked with, and even specific events; but I still can't remember other things. As silly as this may sound—and as I mentioned earlier—I could not even remember the layout of the bathroom in the home I lived in at that time. Some people might think, *Who cares?* For me, it was a big deal. It was another piece to my puzzle, another connection I needed to make.

I later remembered that each day when I got home from the morgue I would get in the shower and cry. I associated the shower with the pain I was feeling, so I disassociated and blocked it out. I recall countless times when trying to remember Doc K saying, "It's okay, just let it go. You might remember, you might not, but it's okay." When I finally just let go and let be, I would recall things more frequently, but as long as I was in a high state of stress when I tried to remember, I got nothing. When I was trying to control my thought process of recall, I was actually blocking it. When I let it go, I often remembered.

I also started recognizing that I was making comments about situations to others, saying things like, "I have no control over that, so I am not going to let it worry me." Again, I was being mindful, just letting things be. The only thing I could (and can) control was *me* and how I react or respond to a given situation. That is the only thing I have control over. When I finally got the concept that I could not control the world around me, my world took on a new peace. This became so important when I began transitioning from my old world to my new one.

When I knew I was being released from the military for medical reasons, I decided to take advantage of the opportunity. I knew deep down that working in the dental profession was not going to be a viable solution to my long-term employment desires. I decided to complete a degree in a field that had been a passion my whole life. Justice.

I enrolled at Royal Roads University in Victoria, British Columbia, in the Bachelor of Justice program. I not only had to complete two years of writing papers and reading but also needed to attend two residency portions. I was nervous and scared. This was basic training all over again—at least mentally.

The first residency was in the middle of my first few months of treatment. My anxiety symptoms were at their peak. To make my situation even more stressful, I would have to fly, I'd be staying on campus, and I'd have to put myself into a mix of strangers. That sounds pretty easy, but when you are dealing with anxiety, none is a task easily ventured. However, if I thought of it in terms of small victories, I could get it done.

I would be lying if I said that entering the room for the meet and greet breakfast the first day was anything short of stomach cramps and nausea. I felt more alone than ever, not to mention that I felt as if I were in high school all over again. It did not take me long to realize that—although many were adults going back to school and we were all in this with the same goal—I was still going to be subjected to petty gossip and cliques. This would become another nemesis of my anxiety, on top of my existing anxiety of having to return back to school.

After the first week, I felt a bit more comfortable. I had rented a car, so I was able to visit with old friends and attend the OSISS support meeting that was scheduled that week. I was not anchored down to the campus, but I was alone. I singled myself out and made myself scarce when we were not in classes. I became my own worst enemy. By the second week, my anxiety intensified when I received a call that my daughter had been in an accident. I immediately called the peer support coordinator from OSISS for his support. I needed to hear that it was okay that I was feeling overwhelmed, and that it was okay if I felt I needed to leave and not attend that third week. He suggested that I speak with my professors to ensure that it was okay that I complete that third week by distance. And that is what I did.

That first year went by quickly. I was still attending my treatment sessions and working on a full curriculum. It was not easy. But I reminded myself about my small victories, things became simpler, and I looked forward to my second residency.

I made a few changes the second year. Rather than stay in residence where I felt uncomfortable, I stayed with my friend Kelly and her family. I found support. I attended the OSISS meeting and reconnected with all my peers. I was able to hear their accomplishments and stories. I found support. I spoke with my husband each day and shared any concerns or triumphs. I found support. I also went for lunch shopping breaks with one of my cohorts, Michelle. It was my time to relax and laugh. But the most important change I made was that I grasped the concept that, regardless of gossip and cliques that existed, I could not control one bit of it. It was not mine to own, so I didn't have to think about it. My only concern was getting to class, teamwork, and assignments.

I am so thankful for the opportunity and the lessons learned from my education journey. By keeping with the plugged-in support, giving up control over things I had no control over, and remembering to be mindful when situations sparked my anxiety, I was able to enjoy and partake in our graduation ceremony in October 2012.

Once I completed my degree, I felt it was time to get back into the grind of work, and boy, have I learned that my ideals and passions have changed. I have discovered that if I am not passionate about what I am doing, I am not willing to sit around and wait for a change to happen. I suppose nearly three years of therapy also provided me an insight to who I am and what has become important. I have learned that I want to utilize my story and situation as a positive factor in life rather than a painful one. I want to share my experience when opportunity exists and educate those who may not quite understand. I want to be able to support and encourage someone else. I want to be someone who is suffering from PTSD's cheering section.

Keeping within the aspects of justice and the valuable lessons and teachings I have learned from my professors at Royal Roads, I am continuing on my road of applying to and completing courses so that I can fulfill my passion of becoming a parole officer or coach of some kind. I want to take my experience and use it to encourage and inspire others to go beyond their stories. I want to work with individuals who may be suffering from mental illnesses such as

PTSD or depression and inspire them to believe and become who they once were before life changed.

Working briefly as a justice of the peace in Calgary—reading bail conditions and other documents to inmates—I became inspired to use my circumstances to help others get beyond theirs. I pondered and thought to myself about how I could make a difference taking what I have gone through and turning it into something positive.

I had recently read an article by a military veteran who is now working within our justice system as a correctional officer. Using his background, he developed and implemented a military-style program for inmates—a program that teaches skills, self-awareness, and self-esteem to those who may have forgotten where such things hide.

As I read the article and read about which military he had previously served with, I thought, *I am sure he has taken his pains of his past and has now used them to inspire others.* It was a true inspiration and validation for me to know that this is the path I was destined for. I truly believe that on September 2, 1998, I was right where I was intended to be. As tragic as the events unfolded were, there have been no coincidences.

Live your life from your heart. Share from your heart. And your story will touch and heal people's souls.—**Melody Beattie**

BLUE SKIES, GREEN GRASS, AND FLUFFY WHITE CLOUDS

Jane Fonda expressed it elegantly during *Oprah's Master Class*. She said, "We were not meant to be perfect. We are meant to be whole." During many years suffering with my symptoms, I tried to be perfect. In my efforts to be perfect, I left out the most important person of all—myself. Somewhere along the way of life, and through many years of serving with the military, I had learned that I could not settle for anything less than perfect—and that if I was not perfect, I was not good enough.

It was not until I began my therapy that I began to discover that I had to take care of the one person for whom I was responsible: me. Up until that point, my ability to set healthy boundaries didn't exist. I was so emotionally numb that my ability was also numb. I closed down my emotions to a point where every negative challenge or situation appeared to be disconnected from my reality. Some days I even felt as if I were not in my body.

I recall stating many times that I felt as if my feet were walking on air. I was battling so many issues at work and home that most days I just wanted to crawl into a small space and go to sleep. I found myself often thinking that I wanted to be left alone. I wanted no part of reality or responsibility. And for many situations where empathy was needed—especially at work—I took on an I-really-don't-care attitude. I lacked compassion for situations and often felt angry. If someone had a personal crisis at home, I closed off from their needs and eventually became the same people who had been emotionally disconnected from my needs. I had mimicked the very personalities that I despised in the past. I not only expected *my* perfection, I expected perfection from others.

It was not until 2005 that I truly began to realize and connect with the fact that I was not well emotionally and physically. My symptoms worsened, and as a result I began insisting that things be investigated. At one point, I recall being placed on medical stress leave.

I discovered very early that I needed to set boundaries, but boundaries were not always well received by others—especially when it came to setting healthy boundaries with family and my work. This was more apparent in my working environment. After being placed on stress leave, I very vividly remember receiving a call from my supervisor stating that he had found me a placement on a very important career course that I required for promotion and that it was starting that week. In that moment, I remember thinking, *Are you kidding me? I just dropped off my medical chit placing me on stress leave.* I was furious. I am not sure where I mustered the strength, but something inside me said, *Just say no.* It's amazing how powerful one two-letter word can be, yet it's the same word that can make us feel so guilty when we are trying to be perfect. The point is, I found it and realized that in that moment, I needed to take care of myself.

I bounced in and out of these self-care strong moments many times throughout the years to follow, but I never lost sight of its concept. I think once I had relived a taste of my own emotional strength and the need to care for myself, I realized, *Enough is enough.*

My next *enough* started to surface in 2007 and then again in 2009. I was faced with situations where I felt like a raccoon backed into a corner by a bully raccoon. It was at that point that I, without a doubt, understood that if I did not stand up for myself, no one else would. It was like the blinders were taken off and I could see others with clarity. I realized that they had only one clear vision, and I was just an employee. The more my passion for the needs of others and myself returned, the more I realized that I needed to make a change—or be sucked back into the vortex of the storm. It was at that moment that I decided that, in the interest of my health and happiness, it was time to leave the military.

As I previously mentioned, sometimes when I set healthy boundaries for myself, those boundaries are not well received by others. This was also true within my family. My daughter, who was still living at home, had a difficult time grasping that Mom was not always going to be available at a moment's whim. I met resistance. She was so comfortable with my old behaviors and habits that personal boundaries were foreign to her. Our relationship seemed to become strained, but I could not let myself get meshed back into old habits by guilt. I knew I had to stay true and stay strong. I know that she would eventually see the change as a positive and that things would get better.

My approach when setting my personal boundaries came from a place of love, not selfishness. Somewhere I had learned that taking care of myself meant I was being selfish. I quickly learned that *not* taking care of myself was selfish.

Healthy boundaries harbored love and caring for others, while I strived to be the best person I could be for both them and me. I needed to be that *whole person*. My boundaries were set in areas of self-care, and I needed to be available for all my medical and recreational appointments. I clearly indicated that I would be attending my appointments. I had to express, especially to my daughter, that her agenda would now have to take my agenda into consideration. Mom's taxi service would not be opened during "me time." This boundary and inconvenience to her eventually became her motivation to obtain her license.

I also set clear boundaries around my study time and insisted that when I was studying or had a paper to write, mom and wife would be *off duty*, and everyone would have to fend for themselves during that time. This boundary was a tough concept for my husband. He would be going about his business, and the minute I would sit down and get into writing, that's when he wanted my attention. He would do this in a loving way, but it drove me bananas. I could be available to him for hours, and within minutes of sitting down working on my studies, he was right there. It was hilarious. As frustrating as it was, I would chuckle and think *Oh my goodness, you're like a little kid whose parent has just gotten on the phone.*

Hobbies have been huge on my self-care list, and I needed to take some time to enjoy them. I am huge into karaoke. I love to sing. I am not a great singer, but I enjoy it. Singing relaxes me. Another interest of mine is the area of design, color, and creativity. I had always had a crafty, creative side, but I decided to take a course in home staging and color consulting to expand my interest. I looked for opportunities to volunteer. I decided to volunteer at our local animal shelter and chose to help out in the area of taking photos of the animals for the shelter's website. Through working with the animals, I learned patience. I also developed a passion for photography. I often spent hours taking the animals' photos and panning through hundreds of pictures in search of that one picture that captured the animal's true personality. Volunteering became more than about volunteering; it became my mission to find that animal a new forever home. They say that animals have a therapeutic effect on our health. An animal's love is unconditional, and they are loyal to their owners. I recently heard of dogs being trained to assist with veterans returning from overseas to help with the management of their PTSD symptoms.

    Self-care has also meant discovering what I'm passionate about. Participating in activities allowed me to focus on something rather than myself while I was focusing on myself—if that makes any sense. What I mean by that is I was always focusing on the negative and my anxiety rather than focusing positively on myself by taking care of myself doing something I enjoyed. It has been amazing to discover that—when I am immersed in doing things I'm passionate about—I think so little about symptoms occurring without warning. I am able to get back into the

Eye of the Storm

activity, and I feel much better overall. I am not in turmoil and I quickly return to that peaceful place. The eye of the storm. The place where calm surrounds me.

An activity as simple as taking a walk and noticing the leaves on the trees, the smell of the air, or even the sounds around me is enough to take me from a place of *hectic* to a place of *serene*. I don't worry about being perfect. Perfect is my any given moment in time when I am just being. Just being me.

We are not meant to be perfect. We are meant to be whole.—**Jane Fonda**

THE VICTORY

Out of the darkness she rode,
Upon her faithful steed.
She slay the dragon in the heart
And left him there to bleed.

She wiped her sword and slung it,
Kept on riding through the night.
With only thoughts of the present,
Could she stay strong and win the fight.

Through the thickened cloud and brush,
She saw a glare of light.
Then with a kick to her horse's side,
She rode with all her might.

The light, it got much brighter,
Having faith that she had one.
For victory lay just ahead
As she rode into the sun.

For the dragon was that of fear,
Of memories too painful to swallow.
And the sun was that of hope,
Facing each as a brighter tomorrow.

Copyright 1991, Jacquie Buckley
Revised 2013, Jacquie Buckley

SEVEN LI'L TIDBITS OF ENCOURAGEMENT

1. Journaling has been a great way for me to express myself emotionally while allowing my thoughts to heal my wounds. Journaling has been a huge process in my healing—a process for which I am very grateful. Writing our words and then rereading them allows us to connect to our thoughts and emotions. I have discovered that when I write, it is usually in the process of rereading my thoughts that I will often connect with my emotions and validate that they are real. During the process of writing this book and while editing, I found myself getting tearful at certain parts. This is not a bad thing. It is a tremendous accomplishment for those of us who suffer from PTSD, another small victory. Our emotions have been fragile, yet distant or nonexistent. I believe that when we journal our feelings, things we're grateful for, and thoughts on a daily basis, we connect with our inner selves in a way that allows us to learn

to love ourselves. When we are grateful and express it, we cannot be bitter or angry.

2. I challenge you to get into the habit of taking time each day to express your feelings, thoughts, and things you're grateful for. Make this a small victory. One day at a time, create a habit of goodness for yourself. It's a self-healing process.

3. Each day, think about what you are feeling. If it is morning, journal how you are feeling the minute you get up. Did you wake up happy, sad, angry, indifferent, or anxious? Whatever you are feeling, write it down. Take a moment to reflect on why you might feel this way. I have learned more about my moods over the past three years than the average bear, and I have also gotten to a place where I can connect with that mood and understand what triggered it. If it is a negative emotion, I now know how to correct it—if I want to.

4. The next thing is to write down at least one or two things you are grateful for and write down different things each day. Write down your small victories accomplished the day before, or if you journal at night, then your small victories that day. You will be amazed that if you truly sit and think of what you accomplished, you will realize that your

small-victory list will probably fill your page. Then acknowledge and give yourself credit for those accomplishments

5. Take time for yourself. As hard as this may seem, take at least fifteen minutes for yourself each day and do something you enjoy. Watch your favorite show, get a massage, relax in the tub, write, or go for a walk. Self-care is important. Connect with whatever it is you enjoy. There is good meaning in the phrase "Take time to smell the roses."

6. If you're living in fear of what others think, I challenge you to be strong and stand up for the person you have become through this process. I especially challenge those still serving—or who have served and are suffering in silence. Or those of you who are serving in a profession that witnesses tragic events on a daily basis, and you have ignored your emotions or feelings based on what you *think* others will think. You deserve to be at your best. Face your fears and work with them. Stop running from them; they will only follow you. Don't let the fears stop you from taking care of yourself.

7. If you're living with fears and are plagued by memories of an event you encountered, I challenge you to take a look at what those

memories have already done to your life—and how they have already changed you. Are they holding you back from getting treatment? Are those fears holding you back from living a normal life of happiness? A happiness that you deserve? Would you rather be miserable for the rest of your life and live in the storm of turmoil and chaos just because you're afraid to get in touch with your emotions? You owe it to yourself to seek assistance and get support to help you control the anxiety and fear that feeds on you.

About the Author

Jacquie is dedicated to others who suffer from posttraumatic stress disorder by helping and encouraging them in their healing journey. She served in the Canadian Forces from 1990 until 2010, when she was released for medical reasons. She worked as a dental hygienist and achieved the rank of sergeant by the time of her release. In pursuit of her passion and her never-ending love for self-growth and learning, she graduated from Royal Roads University in October 2012 with a bachelor's degree in justice studies. She is a mom of two and a grandmother of two. She resides in a small rural community east of Calgary, Alberta, with her husband, two dogs, and a cat.

If you are interested in contacting her to speak, she can be reached by contacting her at negotiatingconflict.com.

About the Artist (Cover)

Clarissa resides on Vancouver Island in the beautiful community of Sooke with her parents and her dog Bailey. She is a high school student and just recently returned from France as part of a school exchange program. Clarissa is fluent in French and English. Her parents both serve

Jacqueline Buckley, CD, BA

in the Canadian Forces. She enjoys hanging out with her friends and sketching. Clarissa's artistic talent can often be seen on the popular website Deviant Art. Her artistic channels go beyond the pen, as she also plays piano.

NOTES